Dear Diary,

Bobbie Hall

BookLeaf Publishing

Dear Diary, © 2023 Bobbie Hall

All rights reserved.

No part of this publication may be reproduced, stored in a retrieval system, or transmitted, in any form or by any means, electronic, mechanical, photocopying, recording or otherwise, without the prior written permission of the presenters.

Bobbie Hall asserts the moral right to be identified as author of this work.

Presentation by *BookLeaf Publishing*

Web: www.bookleafpub.com

E-mail: info@bookleafpub.com

ISBN: 9789357212229

First edition 2023

DEDICATION

For Charlie x

Dear Diary,

What happens to the days that we cannot
remember? It has never sat comfortably with
me.
All of the walks, the cuddles, the jokes that split
our sides but can't recall the punch line.
The new facts that we learn, but who was the
teacher?
The moments that shatter us, build us and make
us.
I decided to write them down.
These are memories we all watch in our minds,
slightly more out of focus with each replay.
The firsts and the lasts, the hello's and the
goodbyes.
Dear Diary,
you have been my safe space, my self soother,
my confessional.
The words in your pages are not coated in sugar,
the poetry doesn't live there.
Your words are heavy and hard and raw.
Because that's what life is.
It's messy.
It's one page bursting with love and laughter,
and another laced with heat and hurt.
You hold the thoughts my mind hadn't yet made
sense of,

You are home to the ink of my heart.
You carry the lost days.

Deep sleep

I wonder why it is that I sleep so soundly now
And I think it's because the darkness is no
longer lonely.
When I stir in the night, there is comfort in
knowing that you are awake over there, going
about your day.
There is no suffocation in the still silence of the
moonlight. And though I cannot touch you, you
are at the end of my fingertips.
I picture what it is that you may be doing and
envy whoever may be close to you.
But if this is the depth of my slumber whilst I
lay half the world away,
I fear when next you,
I may not wake at all.

Faith

Don't lose faith. Always believe that what is meant for you won't pass you by and know that keeping your heart open is a bold and beautiful thing to do. There is bravery in believing in a love that will set your soul on fire. And if you see potential of that then chase it. There is no pride in hiding your feelings away in the shadows. If you see a glimmer of magic then trust yourself enough to follow it. Life is fragile and finite and the only person that can navigate what happens is you. To love loudly is a super power, and what you put into the universe, the universe shall return. So tell people how you feel and let the light shine in. And I promise when you find it, you will know. There will be no doubt, no little voice, no wonder. When the right person comes along you will feel the noise in your head clear like storm clouds after rain. You'll feel yourself fit with them so perfectly, it's like they were made to measure. Oh and how you'll laugh. It will be a new laugh. It's hearty and heavy and full. It comes without warning and sometimes you won't be able to stop it. The type of laugh that can turn silent, only measured by the movement of your shoulders and the tears in your eyes. Always trust in your gut. Don't waste time trying to fit puzzle pieces that do not match. The universe knows. And the universe has your back.

Ocean

Man of the ocean, why do you love it?
What do you feel when the waves touch your
skin?
Is it the depth that speaks to you as you wonder
what lies beneath?
Or the crackling of the salt that dries to your
body?
Is it the vastness that you surrender to?
Or the respect for the current that you cannot
control?
And who do you think of when you stare out to
sea?
Because I always see you,
And I hope you see me.

Poet

You wouldn't be called a chef if you could only
make one dish.
So how is possible to call myself a poet,
When the only words that ever leave my finger
tips
Are the inner thoughts of you?

A little life

It was a life within a life, and what a nice life it
was.
It was young, and fun and pure.
We were told life is long, and he was right. But
too long for us.
Our paths head in different directions now, but I
hope you're facing the sun.
It was our little life.
And what a nice life it was.

Phases of the moon

It's not true, that we only live once.
I have been through many.
And like the phases of the moon, some more
shadowed than the last.
But there are no crescents here.
It's with you,
In this life,
The moon is full.

With you

I'll be with you on the good days, the birthday's
and the Christmasses.
To share bubbly and whisky with you on the seal
of a deal.
I'll be there in the morning to share cups of
coffee, and to fill your belly on an evening.
I'll stand by you when things get tough, through
the losses, the sickness and grief.
I'll even be there when you don't want to talk,
I'll be there waiting. I'll be there.
We'll be together for their first birthday, the
graduations and the weddings.
We'll share in pride as our babies grow tall, and
clever and loving and kind.
And one day we'll be back to just us. Traveling
again, perhaps a little slower this time.
Our hair will become grey, our skin all wrinkled,
but my hand will remain in yours.
And when the light comes and then goes out,
and we turn into dust,
We'll float through the sky and into the next life
and it should come as no surprise,
That I'll be with you there too.

Eggs on toast

Already longing for the simplicity of me and
you,
Salty kisses
And eggs on toast.

10,559

I've just checked the map again to count the
miles between us
10,559
You're asleep but I wish I was there,
holding your hand, with our legs entwined,
Or my lips kissing the back of your head.
I'd tell you things you've heard me say before,
like how I can't believe I've finally found you,
And how lucky we have been.
We would talk about all the plans that we have
and oh babe, the places we'll go.
And when I look at you I'll see the face I've
always dreamt of, but never seen.
It was you.
It was always you.

Sundown

And now, dinner feels so silent.
After a life of rising with the sun,
It's sundown that stirs me
As I sit with you by moonlight.

Manchester

It was solo cocktails at Schofields
And Macbook movies on the mezzanine
Whiskey lock ins in damp smelling pubs,
And boys with wet socks.

It was glasses oysters and fizz outside the
butchers,
And eating tapas in the rain.
A book club, where we read no books
And by the end we could barely read at all.

It was home and then heartbreak and hell.
And heavy, then wholesome, then home again.
Rooftop wines, in fact wine everywhere.

Oh how those cobbles,
Rebuilt me from the rubble.

Life saver

I never knew I needed saving.
But I want you to know that you have saved my
life.
Not from death.
But from mediocrity
And whatever greyscale life it would have been
without you in it.

Because of you

I had always been a believer in love, perhaps it was the books I read a little too young, the films I watched or the way I always heard the lyrics of a song before the music. I believed in a love that was long lasting, that was loud and full of laughter. There were times, I thought I'd found it. But after each chip and heartache I started to believe that type of love wasn't on the cards for me. I'd missed my chance and I had forfeited my right to the fairy tale.
I was wrong.
Darling, now that I have met you and once again believe that we are all deserving of a love that makes us feel safe enough to wear those weighty words on our sleeve; I know that this love is there for all of those that are patient enough to seek it.
There is a love that leaves no doubts. It's a love that will keep you up at night, in order to squeeze every last moment. A love that will take your mind to countries you'd previously never planned on going, and reconnecting with the things you love the most.
Because of you I am full of light and joy, and it's a light that doesn't dim when the doors are

closed. I feel courage, and I spent years not
always feeling so brave.
This is a love that feels unbeatable, that makes
us forget where we are. That I can feel from just
the way you look at me, and that I know we both
can feel from the other side of the world.
The affection I feel for you goes beyond what I
have read in poems but of course,
I now too struggle to find the words.

2am

There is love in the darkness of 2am phone calls
Nightmares lined with silver
Heavy eyes but full hearts
In waiting there is hope
But the days move slow
And when morning comes there is lust
Distance blocked desires.
Floating from dusk 'till dawn.

Hello

In meeting you
I've finally said 'Hello' to me.

Reason

I was told it was you in how peacefully I slept next to you. That first night it was as if my body knew before my mind. And even after that, my heart knew before my mind.

All the distortion that usually hazed my mind, now gone. It felt like the relief you get when you take your bra off after a long day. Or those first few moments in a hot bath. Warm, comforting, peaceful.

It wasn't loud or electric, though of course that all came later. You instantly felt familiar, I could have sworn I had seen that face before, using the similarities between you and a hollywood actor as a cover for the fact I knew it went much deeper than that.

You, my love, have been mapped out on my path since before I was even a twinkle in my mothers eye. The hands that life has dealt me, the joy and the pain all lead me to you on that hot summer evening.

And it's finally now, after years of confusion and soul searching that I realise that the phrase I had always hated to hear came through. The words that would make me recoil in anger

'Everything happens for a reason'

In fact, those words are true.

There always was a reason, and that reason,

Was you.

Forever

For all the times you haven't heard it,
Felt it,
Gave it,
There will be no rations here.

I love you daily,
Hourly,
Fiercely.

I love you with no control,
No pace,
No Patience.

I love you for your heart,
Your humour,
Your soul.

I love you for the eyes that see me as I have
always wanted to be seen. The person I once lost
along the way.

I will hold you with both hands,
Tightly
Forever.

We will bask in glory with our family,
Yours
Mine.

I love you on all of the days
The joyful
The painful.

For I have loved you in all our lives,
Past
Present
Beyond.

Regret

You can be a good person and still fuck up. Please rid yourself of the pressure that we must be perfectly behaved at all times. There is not a single good person on the planet who lives without regret. Regret and guilt are the emotions that make us functioning and empathetic human beings. They mean we care and reflect and have a moral compass. But we musn't hold on to them for too long. Understand those moments, learn from them and grow from them but feel safe in the knowledge that like a phoenix, we can too rise from our own ashes.

Home

To sip coffee in Paris
Or eat pasta in Milan.
Tapas in Barcelona,
And coconuts in Thailand.

I want margaritas in Mexico
To shout 'Opa!' in Greece.
Feel the snow up in the Alps,
Portuguese sand beneath my feet.

But of all the places I want us to go,
Norway, Berlin, Or Rome.
No place will ever beat your chest,
It's your heart that is my home.

www.ingramcontent.com/pod-product-compliance
Lightning Source LLC
LaVergne TN
LVHW021358200726

843509LV00014B/2908